THE WEIGHT OF MY PURPOSE

What Life Took From Me – and What I chose to Carry

Coach Jay (Jayw K. Jackson)

Coach Jay (Jayw K. Jackson) Publishing

Copyright Page

The Weight of My Purpose

What Life Took From Me — and What I Chose to Carry

Copyright © 2026 by Coach Jay (Jayw K. Jackson)

All rights reserved.

No part of this book may be reproduced, stored in a retrieval system, or transmitted in any form or by any means—electronic, mechanical, photocopying, recording, or otherwise—without prior written permission of the publisher, except for brief quotations in reviews.

This book is a work of nonfiction based on the author's life experiences. Some names, locations, and identifying details have been changed to protect the privacy of individuals. Any resemblance to actual people, living or deceased, is coincidental.

"In all your ways acknowledge Him,

and He will make your paths straight."

— Proverbs 3:6 (NIV)

Scripture quotations are taken from the Holy Bible, New International Version® (NIV®). Copyright © 1973, 1978, 1984, 2011 by Biblica, Inc. Used by permission. All rights reserved worldwide.

ISBN: 979-8-9947799-3-4

Printed in the United States of America

Dedication

To God—

who carried me when I couldn't stand,

who stayed when I doubted,

and who held my purpose

even when I thought I'd lost everything.

To my brother—

gone too soon,

but present in every step I take,

every promise I keep,

and every legacy I carry forward.

To my mother—

for your strength, your prayers,

and your love that never wavered,

even when the road was heavy.

And to everyone who showed up for me—

in silence and in struggle,

in faith and in patience,

and who continues to walk with me through the journey.

This book exists because you did.

Author's Note

I didn't write this book because I had everything figured out.

I wrote it because I lost what I thought defined me—and had to learn how to carry purpose without the things I once depended on. Strength. Certainty. Control.

This book is for anyone who's ever felt broken by life and wondered who they were supposed to be afterward.

For a long time, I believed consistency was enough. If I showed up, worked hard, and stayed disciplined, purpose would eventually reveal itself. But life has a way of interrupting our plans. A car accident took my mobility. Grief took my brother. And in those seasons, faith didn't feel strong—it felt questioned.

What I learned is that purpose isn't something you chase when everything is going right. It's something you're forced to carry when everything goes wrong.

The pages that follow aren't about success or branding or building an empire. They're about rebuilding identity after loss. About learning that strength can look like stillness. That faith can exist alongside doubt. And that legacy isn't measured by what we accumulate, but by who we're willing to become for others.

I share this story not as an expert, but as a witness—to pain, to perseverance, and to grace that carried me even when my belief wavered. If any part of this book reminds you that you're still here for a reason, then it has done its job.

You're not behind.

You're not finished.

And what you're carrying still matters.

— Coach Jay

Table of Contents

Prologue — Before the Weight

Chapter 1 — The Crash (The Storm Before the Sunrise)

Chapter 2 — The Seed of Purpose

Chapter 3 — The Leap of Faith

Chapter 4 — The Grind

Chapter 5 — The Team Arrives

Chapter 6 — The Rise

Chapter 7 — The Empire

Chapter 8 — The Promise to My Brother

Chapter 9 — The Legacy

Epilogue — The King's Message

Prologue — Before the Weight

Before the crash, I thought I was solid.

Not perfect — just untouchable in my own way.

I showed up. I worked. I stayed consistent. And in my mind, consistency was the same thing as growth.

I didn't ask for help.

I didn't ask for guidance.

I didn't listen well.

I mistook stubbornness for strength and confidence for clarity. If something didn't make sense to me, I ignored it. If someone tried to correct me, I smiled and kept doing things my way. I wasn't reckless — just uncoachable. Certain that eventually, life would line up because I was putting in the work.

I had discipline without direction.

Momentum without meaning.

From the outside, it looked like progress. Inside, it felt like drifting.

I wasn't lost — just floating.

Going with the flow.

Waiting for something to click.

People would ask me what I wanted next. Where I saw myself going. What my purpose was. I'd give safe answers. Vague ones. I told myself there was no rush. Purpose would come when it came.

I didn't realize that comfort can be a quiet form of stagnation

I was strong. Healthy. Moving forward. And somehow… still avoiding the deeper work. The questions that don't show up on schedules or checklists. The kind you can't outwork.

I thought purpose was something you found — not something you were called into.

Then life interrupted my rhythm.

Not with a warning.

Not with a conversation.

But with a collision that would force me to stop moving long enough to finally see.

The crash didn't break me.

It woke me up.

Chapter 1 — The Crash (The Storm Before the Sunrise)

The night was calm.

Just another drive home.

Streetlights glowed like tired angels, and the only sound was the hum of tires against asphalt. I'd driven this road a hundred times—same route, same rhythm, same quiet prayer whispered under my breath.

"Lord, get me home safe."

Then—

a flash.

The scream of metal.

And silence.

The world spun and folded into darkness.

When I woke up, it wasn't to chaos or shouting. It was the steady, almost mocking beep of a hospital monitor. My vision blurred. My body felt distant—heavy, unresponsive.

I tried to move.

Nothing.

A drunk driver had crossed the line. One mistake. One moment. And my life had been rewritten without my permission.

I was a soldier. A veteran. A man built on discipline and order. I'd faced war, pressure, uncertainty—but never weakness like this. Now I couldn't lift my leg. Couldn't grip a dumbbell. Couldn't stand without pain slicing through every nerve.

For days, the loudest thing in the room wasn't the machines—it was my own mind.

Why me?

What now?

What's left?

Family came. Friends stopped by. Their faces were full of hope, encouragement, prayers. But when the room emptied and the lights dimmed, I stared at the ceiling and talked to God like He was the last friend I had left.

"You took my strength," I whispered. "What do You want me to do now?"

And deep inside that silence, something answered—not loud, not dramatic, but certain.

"I didn't take your strength. I'm about to redefine it."

I didn't understand what that meant yet. But something shifted. A small crack opened in the fear. A realization I wasn't ready to name.

Months passed. Rehab became my new battlefield. Every movement was a war. Every stretch, a mission. Doctors told me I'd walk again—but not the same.

I smiled through clenched teeth.

"I wasn't made to be the same."

Each day, I wrote in a small notebook beside my bed. Not about pain—but about purpose. Not about what I lost—but about what I could rebuild.

One night, flipping through those pages, I stopped at a phrase I'd written months before the crash—something pulled from an old journal, almost forgotten.

Live fit — in body, mind, and spirit.

I underlined it twice.

I didn't know it then, but the crash wasn't the end of my story.

It was the interruption I didn't ask for and the awakening I didn't know I needed.

What felt like loss was actually weight — the kind that forces you to grow stronger or collapse under it.

That night didn't take my purpose from me. It made room for it.

Chapter 2 — The Seed of Purpose

Hospitals can feel like prisons when you're used to movement.

For a man who lived by motion—early mornings, late nights, always pushing—the stillness felt suffocating. I'd sit by the window, sunlight dripping through half-closed blinds, watching people walk freely across the parking lot. Each step they took reminded me of what I'd lost.

But beneath the frustration, another thought began to whisper.

You still have something left.

It started with memories of the soldiers I used to train. How I pushed them past their limits. How their bodies changed—but their minds transformed first. I remembered the look in their eyes the moment they realized they were stronger than they thought.

That moment was what I missed most.

I didn't just want to move again.

I wanted to inspire movement.

So I started sketching—not pictures, but ideas. On a crumpled napkin from my hospital tray, I wrote three words:

Live Fit Athletics.

Simple. But heavy with meaning.

Live—because surviving isn't the same as living.

Fit—because strength starts in the mind before it shows in the body.

Athletics—because life itself is a test of endurance.

I didn't know how it would happen or when. But I knew why. God didn't bring me through that wreck just to leave me sitting still. There was a mission attached to the miracle.

Months later, after therapy sessions that tested my patience more than my pain tolerance, I stood again—shaky, slow, determined. When the doctor told me I'd walk with a limp for the rest of my life, I smiled.

"Then I'll limp into my destiny."

I started visiting small gyms—not to work out, but to observe. Trainers shouting without connection. People lifting with no direction. Bodies moving, minds absent.

They were strong.

But they were lost.

That's when the vision sharpened.

A gym that trained the mind as much as the body.

A space where broken people could rebuild themselves.

Where "fit" meant more than abs—it meant alive.

I saved every dollar I could. Sketched logos late into the night. Read business books. Watched sermons. Prayed over plans. Some nights, I fell asleep at the kitchen table with my Bible open and a half-written mission statement beside it.

Every night ended the same way.

"Lord, let this be bigger than me."

I didn't realize it then, but purpose doesn't show up when you're winning. It's born in the quiet after loss—when you stop asking why me and start asking what now.

Slowly, pain turned into direction.

The dream found structure.

And the man who once begged to walk again began planning how to lead again.

Chapter 3 — The Leap of Faith

The air smelled like dust and paint thinner.

The building was old—cracked concrete floors, flickering lights, graffiti telling the story of a neighborhood long forgotten.

But to me, it wasn't broken.

It was blank.

This was where Live Fit Athletics would be born.

No investors.

No ribbon-cutting ceremony.

Just a veteran, a vision, and a prayer.

I used the last of my savings to sign the lease. People told me I was crazy.

"Gyms fail every day," they said.

But when God gives you a vision, logic has to sit down.

I swept the floors myself. Scrubbed the mirrors. Painted the walls black and green—colors of power and purpose. The first weights I bought were mismatched, rusty, and secondhand. When I stacked them on the rack, I smiled.

They looked like hope wearing metal.

Every corner of that gym carried a piece of me—the pain, the prayers, the patience.

I didn't have marketing money, so I passed out flyers by hand. I didn't have fancy machines, so I taught people how to train with grit instead of gadgets. Every client who walked through the door, I treated like family—because I remembered the days when no one showed up for me.

The first day we opened, forty-one people came.

By the second week?

Seven.

One night, I sat alone on a bench with the lights off, counting the few dollars in a jar. Rent was due. Bills were stacking up. I put my head in my hands and whispered,

"Lord, I did everything You asked. Why isn't it working?"

Then came a voice—not loud, but heavy.

"Because I'm not building your gym. I'm building you."

I sat there for hours, tears soaking into my palms. When I finally stood up, something shifted. It wasn't about money anymore. It wasn't about crowds or numbers.

It was about changing one person at a time.

So I went back to work.

I trained a high school kid for free. Helped a single mom lose fifty pounds. Helped a retired vet walk without pain. Word started to spread—not about a gym, but about a man who cared.

People didn't just come to sweat.

They came to heal.

Little by little, Live Fit Athletics became more than a place.

It became a movement.

One day, a client looked at me and said, "You didn't just train my body, Coach—you fixed my faith."

That night, I sat in my car with my hands on the steering wheel and cried again.

This time, it was gratitude.

I didn't know it then, but faith doesn't always start with fire. Sometimes it begins with failure. The leap was never about knowing where I would land—it was about trusting who would catch me.

The gym was never the dream.

It was the assignment.

Chapter 4 — The Grind

Before the fame, before the followers, before the merch—there was the grind.

The kind nobody saw.

I woke up before the sun, knees stiff from the accident, my body aching from old injuries. I prayed, stretched, and poured a cup of black coffee that tasted like ambition and perseverance. Then I unlocked the gym while the city was still asleep.

The sound of the key turning in the door became my morning anthem—a reminder that no matter what life tried to break, I still had control over my effort.

There were days when the lights barely worked. Nights when the AC failed and sweat turned the floor slick beneath my feet. I trained clients, cleaned bathrooms, balanced the books, and built my dream one rep at a time.

I wasn't chasing followers.

I was chasing faithfulness.

Some nights, I collapsed on the gym floor, staring at the ceiling fans spinning like time itself. My body was exhausted, but my spirit was alive. Every day, someone new walked through the door and said,

"Coach, I heard what you're doing here. I need help."

And that was enough.

I learned quickly that purpose doesn't pay you right away—it tests you first. There were weeks when the bills stacked higher than my deadlift. Times when I had to choose between new gym mats or my own dinner.

Every time, I chose the gym.

I wasn't just building a business.

I was building a movement.

I started documenting the journey—short videos of workouts, conversations about life, moments of honesty. No filters. No scripts. Just truth. People began sharing them, not because of perfection, but because they recognized pain turned into power.

I called it Faith in Motion.

Because every rep, every post, every word carried meaning.

Soon, the message spread beyond the gym walls. Other veterans reached out. Single parents. Students. People who were broken—just like I once was.

They didn't see a trainer.

They saw proof.

Proof that God doesn't call the qualified—He qualifies the called.

One night, after finishing my last client, I walked outside and looked up at the stars. For the first time in years, I didn't feel lost. I whispered,

"Thank You for every no that led me here."

Then I went back inside, wiped the sweat off the mirrors, turned off the lights, and smiled at the words painted on the wall:

LIVE FIT ATHLETICS

Mind. Body. Spirit.

I didn't know it yet, but the grind wasn't punishing me—it was preparing me. Every late night, every lonely morning, every prayer that felt unanswered was laying a brick.

And God does His best work in the dark.

Chapter 5 — The Team Arrives

Every movement starts with one person's conviction.

But even kings need a kingdom.

The gym was growing—slow, steady, solid. What once echoed with silence now pulsed with energy: music blasting, weights clanging, people shouting each other's names in encouragement. Every morning, I walked through those doors nodding to faces that used to be strangers and now felt like family.

Still, I was doing everything alone—marketing, training, cleaning, managing, praying. I didn't realize then that the same God who gave me the dream was already sending the help.

One evening, after finishing a brutal leg session, I heard a voice behind me.

"Coach, if you ever need help around here, I got you."

I turned around and saw a young trainer—hungry, humble, built like a soldier. He reminded me of myself years ago. That night, we talked until the lights went out. Different paths, same purpose.

A week later, two more joined us. One was a nutritionist who had battled depression and found healing through fitness. The other was a former athlete who had lost everything and was looking for a second chance. They didn't come looking for jobs.

They came looking for a mission.

That night, we prayed together on the gym floor—no speeches, no business pitch. Just faith.

"Lord, if this is Your team, make us one body with one purpose."

From that moment, something clicked.

Live Fit Athletics stopped being my dream and became our calling. We started planning small boot camps in the community. We visited schools, churches, and veteran centers, spreading a message of faith, fitness, and family.

People noticed the difference.

This wasn't just another gym.
It was revival with dumbbells.

Then came the moment that changed everything.

A short video we filmed after a group workout went viral. It wasn't polished—the camera was shaky, the lighting was bad—but the message was real.

"We're not just training bodies. We're training warriors."

Thousands of views turned into tens of thousands. People started tagging us, sharing their stories, ordering shirts online. The words Live Fit Athletics began traveling farther than our city ever could.

I looked at my team one day and said,

"We didn't go viral. God did."

They laughed—but deep down, we all knew it was true.

The energy shifted.

The team became family.

The gym became home.

Together, we started planning something bigger than any of us had imagined—not just a gym, but a global brand built on faith, resilience, and community.

One night, we sat around a folding table with takeout boxes, sketching ideas for merch, apparel, and expansion. Someone asked,

"Coach, where do you see this going?"

I smiled.

"Worldwide."

And everyone in the room believed it.

I didn't know it then, but the right people don't just join a vision—they multiply it. God doesn't send a team when you're comfortable. He sends them when you're tired but obedient, when you've proven you'll lead with heart before you lead with hands.

Alignment mattered more than audience.

And we were just getting started.

Chapter 6 — The Rise

It started like a spark.

A post here.

A transformation story there.

Before long, Live Fit Athletics wasn't just a gym—it was a statement.

People began driving in from neighboring cities just to train with us. They didn't come for the equipment. They came for the energy. For the first time in my life, the man who once couldn't stand without help was standing in front of crowds who saw him as inspiration.

I was living the prayers I once cried through.

The walls that used to echo with emptiness now vibrated with purpose. Posters of real clients lined the gym—each one a story of redemption: the veteran who learned to walk again, the mother who reclaimed her strength, the kid who found his confidence.

What started as a handful of shirts in a cardboard box became something bigger. We called it Live Fit Athletics Apparel. Simple designs. Clean messages. It wasn't about fashion—it was about faith in motion.

Orders began coming in from out of state. Then from out of the country. One morning, I opened my email and saw it:

Order Confirmed — London, UK.

I stared at the screen in silence. A man who once couldn't walk across a hospital room now had his vision traveling across oceans.

But success isn't quiet.

It brings noise—both praise and pressure.

Interviews, brand deals, and opportunities started flooding in. Everyone wanted to partner, promote, profit. But not everyone came with purpose. I noticed the fake smiles. The handshakes hiding agendas. The same world that once ignored me was now calling my name.

Sometimes, that praise felt heavier than the pain ever did.

One night, sitting alone in my office, I stared at the Live Fit Athletics logo on the wall and whispered,

"Lord, don't let me forget where I came from."

Because I knew this truth well—success without humility is just another kind of crash.

So I kept serving.

Kept mentoring my team.

Kept giving away free memberships to kids who couldn't afford them.

I remembered what it felt like to have nothing, and I promised myself I'd never let success erase that memory.

The videos started reaching millions of views. Major fitness influencers quoted my words. Magazines reached out for features. But whenever people asked what the secret was, my answer never changed.

"Faith. Discipline. Love."

That simplicity was what made Live Fit Athletics unstoppable.

Because while the world saw a brand,

God saw a ministry.

I learned quickly that the real test of success isn't how high you rise—it's how grounded you stay. Every blessing carries weight. Every level brings new pressure. And the only thing that kept me steady was remembering who this was all for.

I wasn't climbing alone.

And I wasn't climbing for myself.

Chapter 7 — The Empire

The glow of sunrise poured through the glass office windows. Below, the parking lot was packed—not just with cars, but with purpose. People from across the country had come for the first Live Fit Athletics Expo, an event that started as a dream scribbled on a napkin and now filled an arena.

Booths lined the floor: Live Fit apparel, supplements, motivational workshops, fitness challenges. A massive banner stretched across the room, reading:

Build the Body. Strengthen the Mind. Lead the Life.

Backstage, I watched my team move like clockwork—the same people who once swept floors and folded shirts now running departments, leading workshops, and inspiring crowds. I smiled, not out of pride, but gratitude.

I knew exactly where we all came from.

When I stepped onto the stage, the noise was thunder. Phones lifted. Cameras flashed. But what hit me hardest wasn't the attention—it was the faith it took to get there.

I grabbed the mic and paused. Then I said what I'd been saying since day one:

"This isn't about muscles.

This is about mindset.

I was broken, lost, and told I'd never stand again.

But I'm here because pain didn't end me—it trained me."

The crowd erupted—not because it sounded good, but because they felt it. Every tear, every rep, every moment of faith was built into those words.

I looked to my left and saw my team standing together—men and women from different backgrounds, different stories, one purpose. I looked to my right and saw my wife and kids, smiling through tears.

For a moment, everything went quiet.

No music.

No noise.

Just a whisper in my heart:

This is what I was preparing you for.

Months later, Live Fit Athletics became an international powerhouse. Global partnerships. Apparel shipping across continents. A new headquarters—state-of-the-art gym, offices, and a creative studio for content and design.

The world saw an empire.

But I knew the truth.

It wasn't built on money or marketing.

It was built on faith and family.

Every success came with a seed—donations to veteran programs, youth mentorships, fitness scholarships. Every time we shipped an order overseas, I'd say,

"That's not a sale—that's a soul we're reaching."

Because the goal was never wealth.

It was impact.

Even in victory, I kept one hand on the ground—still coaching, still mentoring, still praying before every meeting. One night, over a late dinner, I told my team,

"We're not just building a brand.

We're building a legacy—something our kids' kids can be proud of."

They nodded, because by then they understood.

The empire was never what we built.

It was who we built.

The world measures success in numbers. God measures it in names—the people lifted, healed, and changed along the way. Legacy isn't about leaving something behind.

It's about leaving someone ready to carry it forward.

Chapter 8 — The Promise to My Brother

There are pains the body can recover from.

And then there are the ones the soul carries forever.

Three years ago, the phone rang—and the world went quiet. I remember every detail: the time, the tone, the disbelief that felt like a bad dream I couldn't wake up from.

My younger brother was gone.

Just like that.

We grew up together. Fought together. Laughed through late nights filled with dreams about the future. Back then, we thought we had time—time to build together, time to celebrate success, time to live out everything we talked about in those long conversations full of faith, hunger, and ambition.

It was supposed to be us.

Living.

Winning.

Getting rich together.

But time ran out.

On the day of the funeral, I stood beside the casket staring at the man who used to call me "big bro." My knees felt weak. My chest felt hollow. I didn't cry right away—not because I didn't feel it, but because the pain was too deep for tears.

I leaned in and whispered through trembling lips,

"I'll take it from here, lil bro. I got you."

That became the promise that shaped everything that came after.

In the months that followed, I felt empty. The success of the gym, the merch, the brand—none of it filled that space. Because how do you celebrate when a piece of your soul is missing from the room?

There were nights I wished heaven had a phone.

Just so I could hear his voice one more time.

Just so I could tell him how big his son was getting.

Sometimes I still catch myself thinking, I wish you could meet your nephew.

Then I remember—you already live through him.

I'd walk into the gym and stare at the wall of photos—my team, my clients, my family—and imagine my brother standing there too. Laughing. Coaching. Talking trash the way only brothers can. There were days I almost quit. Days when grief felt heavier than any weight I'd ever lifted.

And then there was the guilt.

Survivor's guilt.

I didn't feel right being happy without him. Smiling felt like betrayal. Winning felt unfair. I'd think, Why do I get to live this life when you don't?

I'm sorry I cry so much.

This shit hurts.

Then I remembered—he left behind a son.

A boy with the same eyes.
The same smile.
The same fire.

One day, I watched my nephew run around the gym, laughing, pointing at the posters, pretending to lift weights. In that moment, something inside me broke—and something else rebuilt.

The mission wasn't just mine anymore.
It wasn't even just for my family.

It was for him.

I made a promise I don't say out loud often—that I'd be the best uncle I could be. That I'd show him the world. That I'd guide him, protect him, and one day buy him his first car.

All of it—for you.

I started bringing my nephew around more. Let him sit in on meetings. Watch workouts. Help fold shirts. Hand out flyers. I taught him the same lessons my brother taught me—about respect, responsibility, and faith.

Every time that boy smiles, I see my brother again.

Not in memory—but in motion.

That's when I understood something I couldn't before.

Death doesn't end legacy.

It multiplies it—if you carry it right.

One night, sitting alone in my office, I opened my Bible. A Live Fit hoodie lay folded beside it. I whispered,

"I lost my brother… but I found my purpose."

I wrote one line in my journal that night:

This isn't just my success. This is our redemption.

The pain never left.
But it was reassigned.

Every rep.
Every sale.
Every speech.
Every expansion.

They all carry his name in spirit.

And the next morning, when my nephew walked into the gym wearing a shirt that read—

LIVE FIT — FOR MY DAD

—I knew the promise was still alive.

My pain became my promise. And my promise became my purpose.

Chapter 9 — The Legacy

The mornings were quieter now.

The alarms that once dragged me out of bed before sunrise had been replaced by soft laughter echoing through the house. My son ran down the hallway with a toy dumbbell in his hand. My daughter sat at the kitchen table, sketching ideas for the next Live Fit collection. My wife—the heartbeat of this journey—brewed coffee and smiled at me like she'd known all along how this would end.

The empire was running itself now.

The gym was full.

The clothing line had gone global.

The foundation was funding scholarships for veterans and young athletes around the world.

But what filled me most wasn't the numbers.

It was the peace.

For the first time since the crash, I wasn't fighting to build.

I was living inside what had already been built.

One afternoon, I walked into the gym—not as Coach Jay the CEO, but as the man who once limped through those same doors with nothing but faith. The air smelled like chalk and ambition. Music played softly in the background. I looked around and saw faces I didn't recognize—trainers I'd never met, clients I'd never spoken to—but they all carried the same energy.

They moved with purpose.

At the center of the gym, a new sign hung on the wall:

LIVE FIT ATHLETICS

The House That Faith Built

I stood there in silence, eyes heavy, heart steady. Everything I thought I'd lost had returned stronger.

My body healed. My faith restored. My family whole.

Later that week, I sat at a long table inside the new headquarters. Around me were my partners, my team, my mentors—and my family. The same people who once showed up with nothing but belief.

In that moment, the circle closed.

A retired veteran, once broken by life, now sat surrounded by a family and a movement designed by God Himself. I smiled and said,

"We didn't just build a brand.

We built believers."

No applause.

No speeches.

Just gratitude.

That night, I took my son for a drive. City lights shimmered against the dark sky. He looked out the window for a long time before asking,

"Dad… are you rich now?"

I laughed.

"I'm richer than I ever thought I'd be."

"Because of the money?" he asked.

I shook my head and spoke softly.

"No, son. Because I didn't quit when I could've. And because now—you'll never have to start from nothing."

That's when I understood what legacy really is.

Not what people remember you for—but what they keep living because of you.

The goal was never fame, followers, or fortune.
It was faith.
Freedom.
Family.

The crash didn't end me.
It crowned me.

The pain didn't break me.
It built me.

And everything that came after was proof that when God rewrites your story, He doesn't make edits.

He makes it mean something.

Epilogue — A Final Word

To whoever is reading this—

You might feel broken.
You might feel lost.
You might believe it's already over.

But trust me—what you're carrying isn't the end.
It's the beginning of your purpose.

Kings aren't born in palaces.
They're forged in the fire.

Live fit.
Live free.
Live faithful.
— Coach Jay

Thank you for reading.

If this book reached you, it did so for a reason. These pages represent one season of my life—written honestly, without trying to impress, explain, or soften the truth. This story ends here, exactly where it was meant to.

If this book resonated with you, I ask that you leave a review wherever you purchased it. Reviews help this story reach people who may need these words at a moment when they feel unseen, unheard, or unsure of their next step. Even a few honest sentences make a difference.

You can stay connected with me on Instagram at **@JayLiveFit_**, where I share reflections, lessons, and updates on future projects.

Book number two is coming soon. It is not a continuation of this story, but a completely different chapter of my life—another perspective, another season, and another truth that deserves its own space.

Thank you for your time, your support, and your willingness to read this season with me.

— Jay Jackson

Support the merch, Tap in : **www.valtremerch.com**

www.ingramcontent.com/pod-product-compliance
Lightning Source LLC
LaVergne TN
LVHW041637070526
838199LV00052B/3407